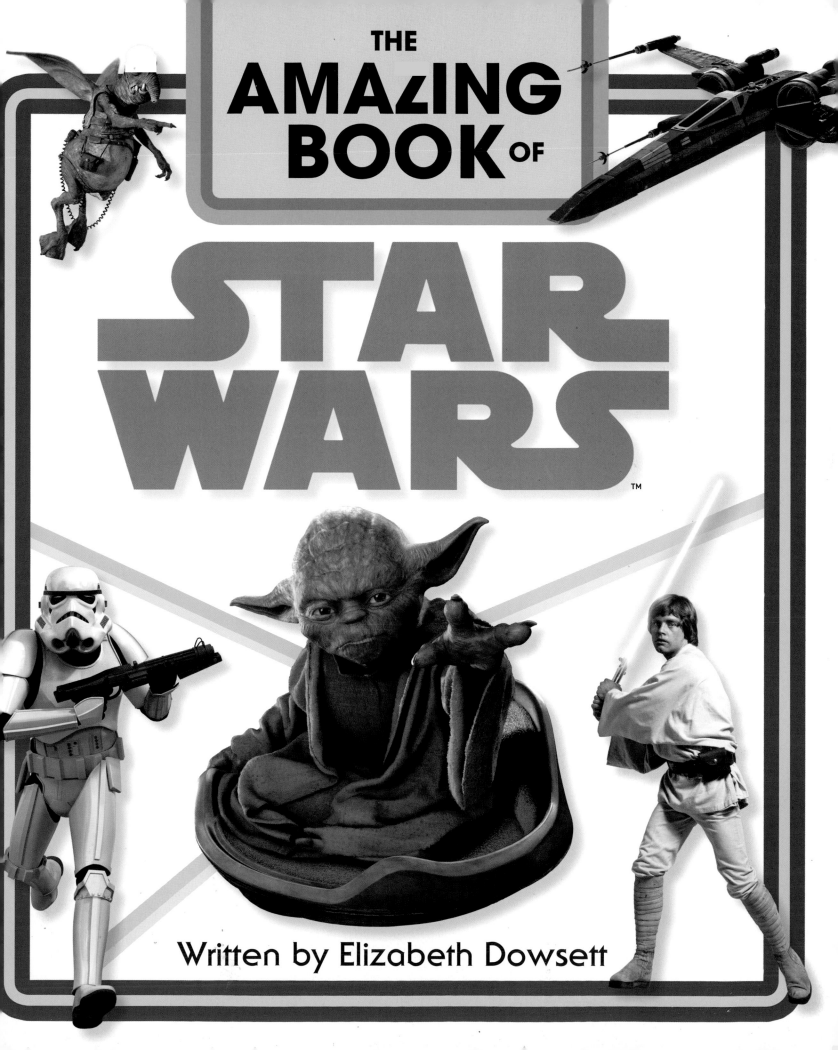

# THE AMAZING BOOK OF

# STAR WARS™

Written by Elizabeth Dowsett

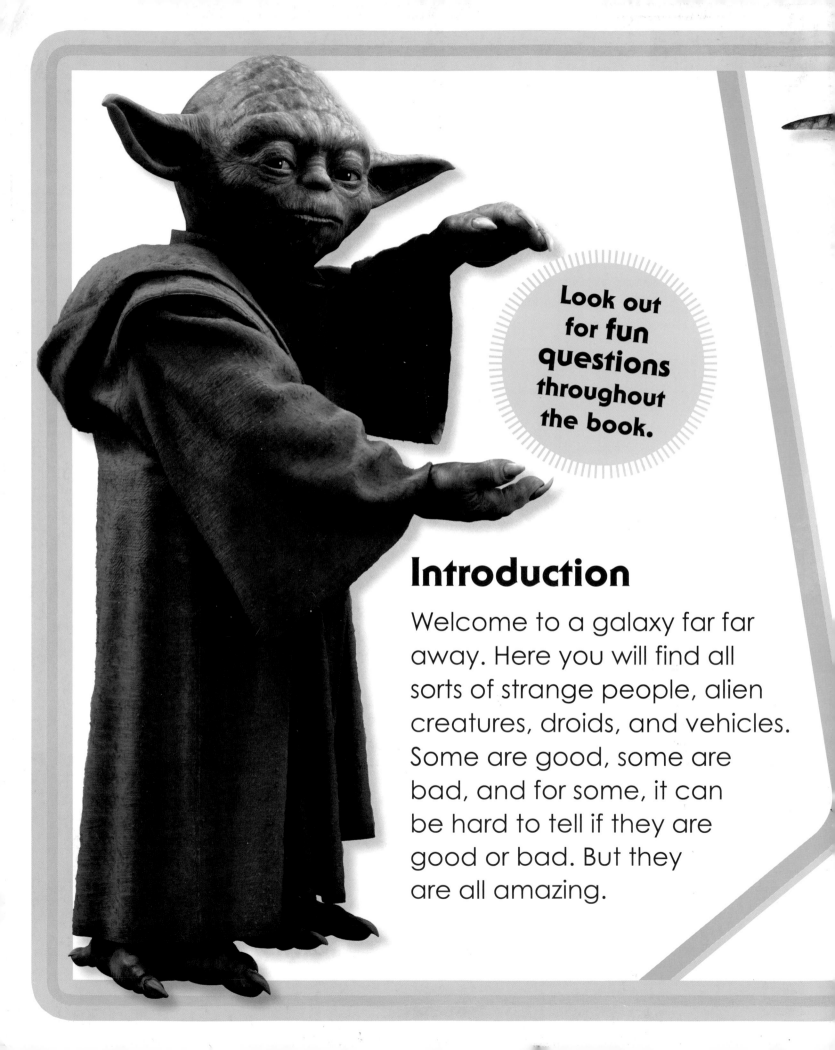

**Look out for fun questions throughout the book.**

## Introduction

Welcome to a galaxy far far away. Here you will find all sorts of strange people, alien creatures, droids, and vehicles. Some are good, some are bad, and for some, it can be hard to tell if they are good or bad. But they are all amazing.

# CONTENTS

# FRIENDLY DROIDS

Which droid rolls like a ball?

Lift the flap to find out!

**Sensor for smelling**

**Electrical wires**

**Oiled knee joint**

## C-3PO

C-3PO is a shiny gold protocol droid. Protocol droids help people understand each other. C-3PO can speak more than six million languages.

**Large green ears**

# Yoda

Wise Yoda is more than 900 years old. Don't be fooled by his small size. He is the most powerful Jedi and the best at lightsaber battles!

**Two-handed grip on lightsaber**

# Mace Windu

All across the galaxy, Mace Windu is respected for his wisdom. When this calm, powerful Jedi talks, people listen.

**Simple Jedi robes**

Antenna receives data

# BB-8

This round astromech droid doesn't walk, he rolls! BB-8 is easily scared, but he always steps up to help out his friends.

**Head spins all the way around**

**Ball-shaped body**

**Tools fold out**

Which is your **favorite droid?**

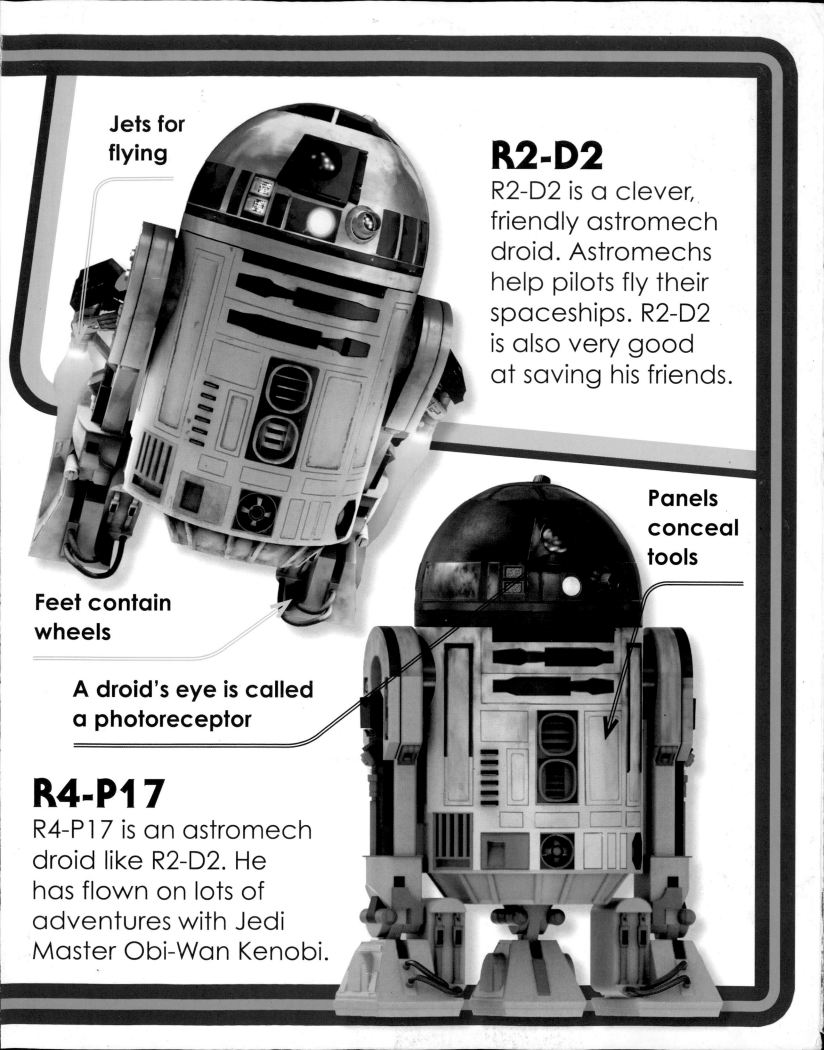

**Jets for flying**

# R2-D2

R2-D2 is a clever, friendly astromech droid. Astromechs help pilots fly their spaceships. R2-D2 is also very good at saving his friends.

**Feet contain wheels**

**A droid's eye is called a photoreceptor**

**Panels conceal tools**

# R4-P17

R4-P17 is an astromech droid like R2-D2. He has flown on lots of adventures with Jedi Master Obi-Wan Kenobi.

# JEDI MASTERS

Headtails

Natural Togruta skin color

## Shaak Ti
Shaak Ti is skilled at fighting. Her hollow headtails sense the space around her so she can duck out of danger quickly.

Kit's lightsaber is waterproof

Head tentacles

## Kit Fisto
Kit Fisto can breathe in air and water. He senses feelings. This makes him a good friend, but also a fearsome warrior.

## Young Anakin
As a child, Anakin Skywalker surprises everyone with his skill with the Force. He loves to fly machines in really fast races called podraces.

Flying goggles

Flying helmet

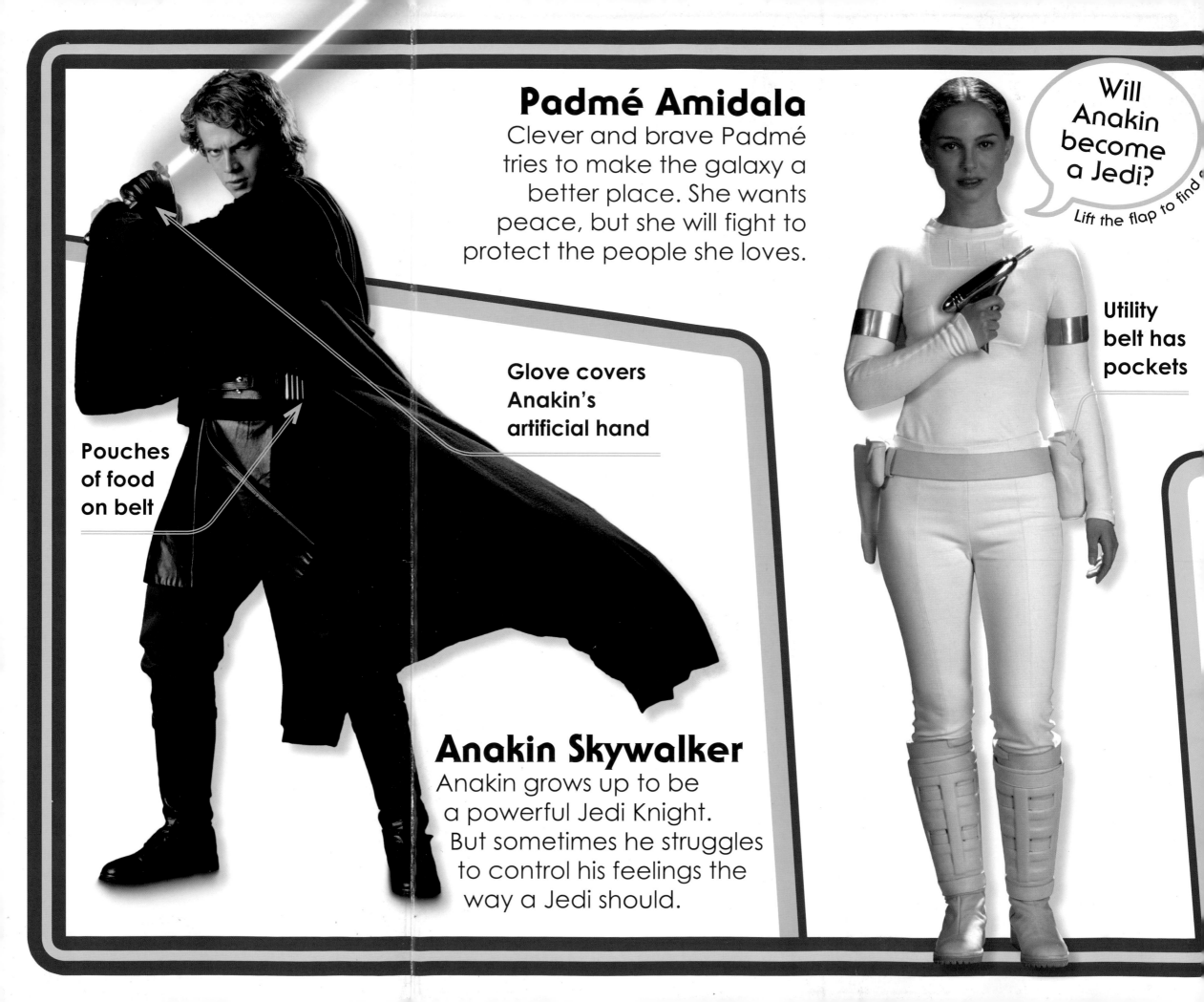

## Padmé Amidala

Clever and brave Padmé tries to make the galaxy a better place. She wants peace, but she will fight to protect the people she loves.

Will Anakin become a Jedi?

Lift the flap to find

Utility belt has pockets

**Glove covers Anakin's artificial hand**

**Pouches of food on belt**

## Anakin Skywalker

Anakin grows up to be a powerful Jedi Knight. But sometimes he struggles to control his feelings the way a Jedi should.

# BRAVE HEROES

Blue blade is powered by a blue crystal

Jedi tunic

Tool belt

## Obi-Wan Kenobi

Wise Obi-Wan Kenobi is Anakin's Jedi Master. He's a skilled warrior, but he prefers to win by using words rather than by fighting.

9

# CLONE SOLDIERS

## Clone Pilot

Clone soldiers who show particular talent are given extra training to become pilots. They fly gunships and spaceships.

**Colored visor**

**Tube carries air**

**Machine helps pilots breathe**

# Clone Trooper

Clone troopers fight with the Jedi to protect the galaxy. They are grown in a factory and are all identical to each other.

**Binoculars**

**DC-15 blaster rifle**

**Basic white armor**

**Would you like to be a clone?**

**Belt with pockets**

...rmor hinged ...o leg ...an bend

# ARC Trooper

A few clones are trained for special missions. They are called ARC troopers and they have red marks on their armor.

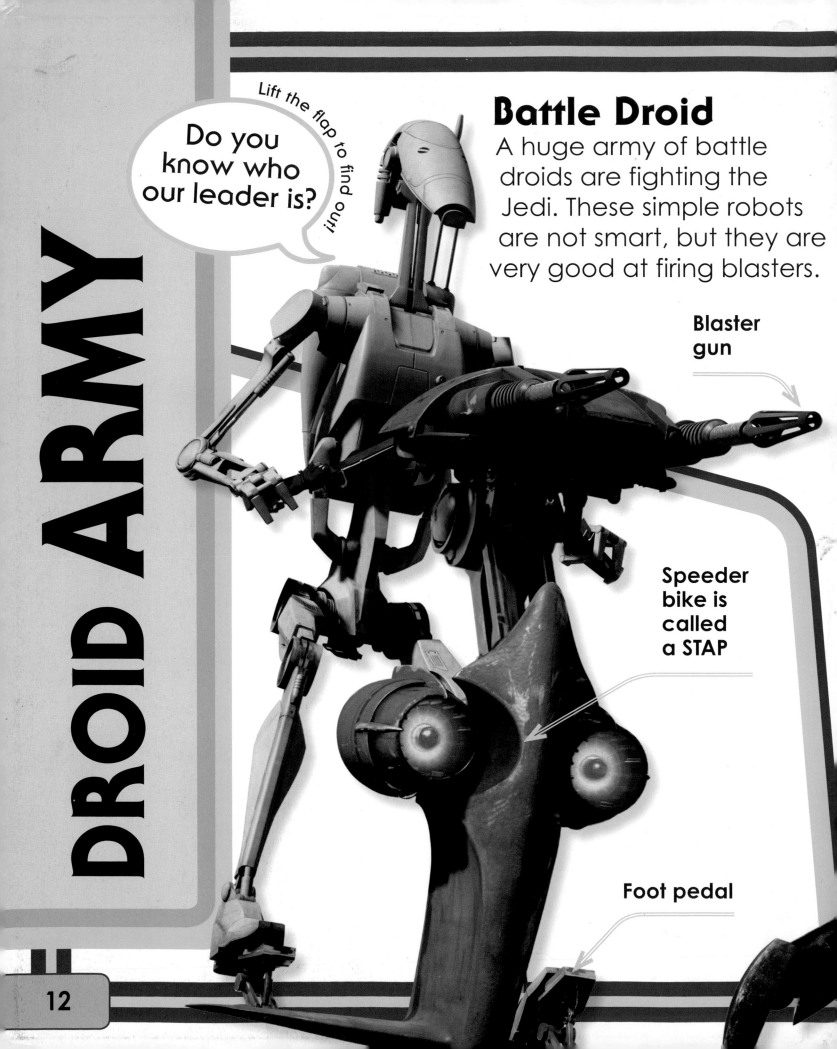

# DROID ARMY

Lift the flap to find out!

Do you know who our leader is?

## Battle Droid

A huge army of battle droids are fighting the Jedi. These simple robots are not smart, but they are very good at firing blasters.

**Blaster gun**

**Speeder bike is called a STAP**

**Foot pedal**

How would **you battle** General Grievous?

Metal skull contains a real brain

Real heart beats inside metal chest

## Droideka

Beware these rolling droids of war! Droidekas wheel onto the battlefield, then uncurl to reveal their deadly blasters.

**Blaster fire**

**Shield for protection**

## Super Battle Droid

Super battle droids are the muscle of the droid army. They are bigger, stronger, and tougher than regular battle droids, but they are no smarter.

**Extra thick armor**

**Blaster bolts shoot from wrist**

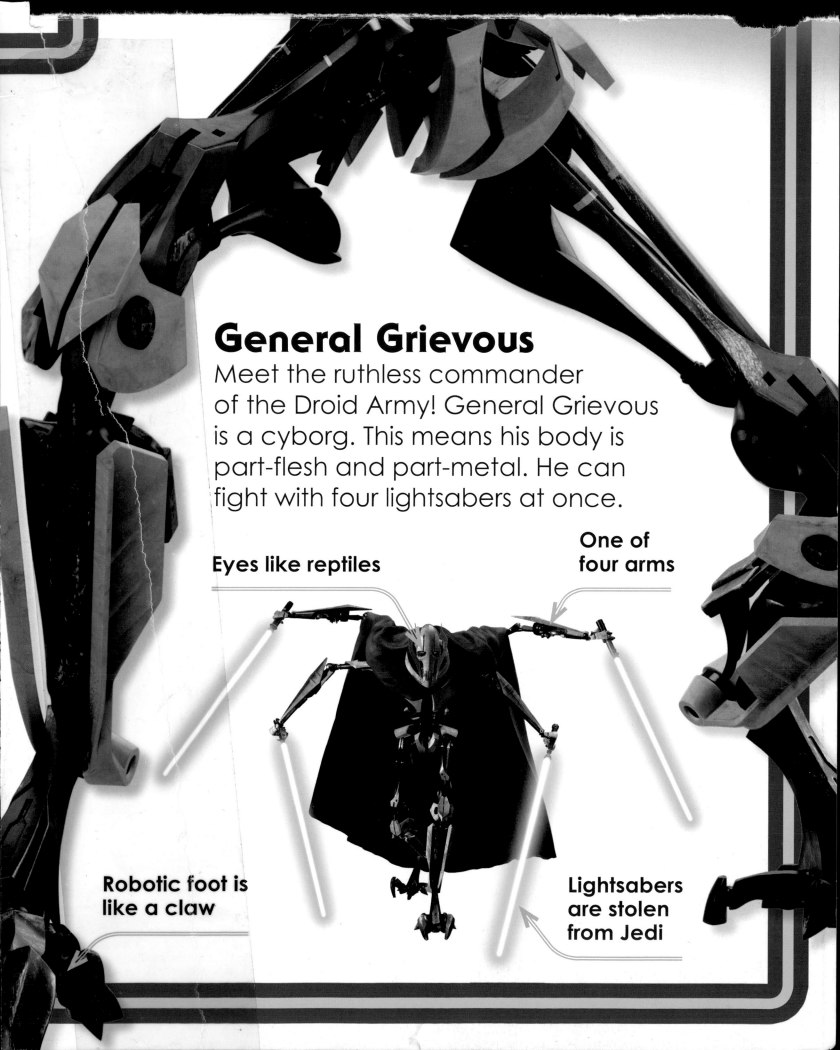

# General Grievous

Meet the ruthless commander of the Droid Army! General Grievous is a cyborg. This means his body is part-flesh and part-metal. He can fight with four lightsabers at once.

**Eyes like reptiles**

**One of four arms**

**Robotic foot is like a claw**

**Lightsabers are stolen from Jedi**

# DANGEROUS DROIDS

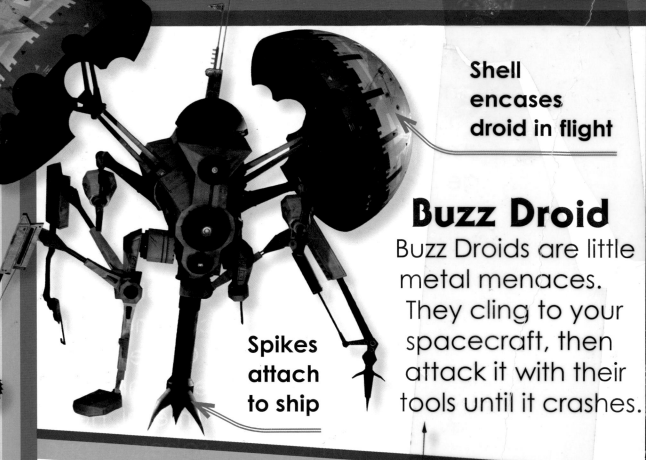

**Shell encases droid in flight**

## Buzz Droid

Buzz Droids are little metal menaces. They cling to your spacecraft, then attack it with their tools until it crashes.

**Spikes attach to ship**

## Dwarf Spider Droid

These four-legged machines scuttle into battle with the Droid Army, armed with a deadly laser cannon.

**Eyes glow red**

**Hinged legs move like a spider's**

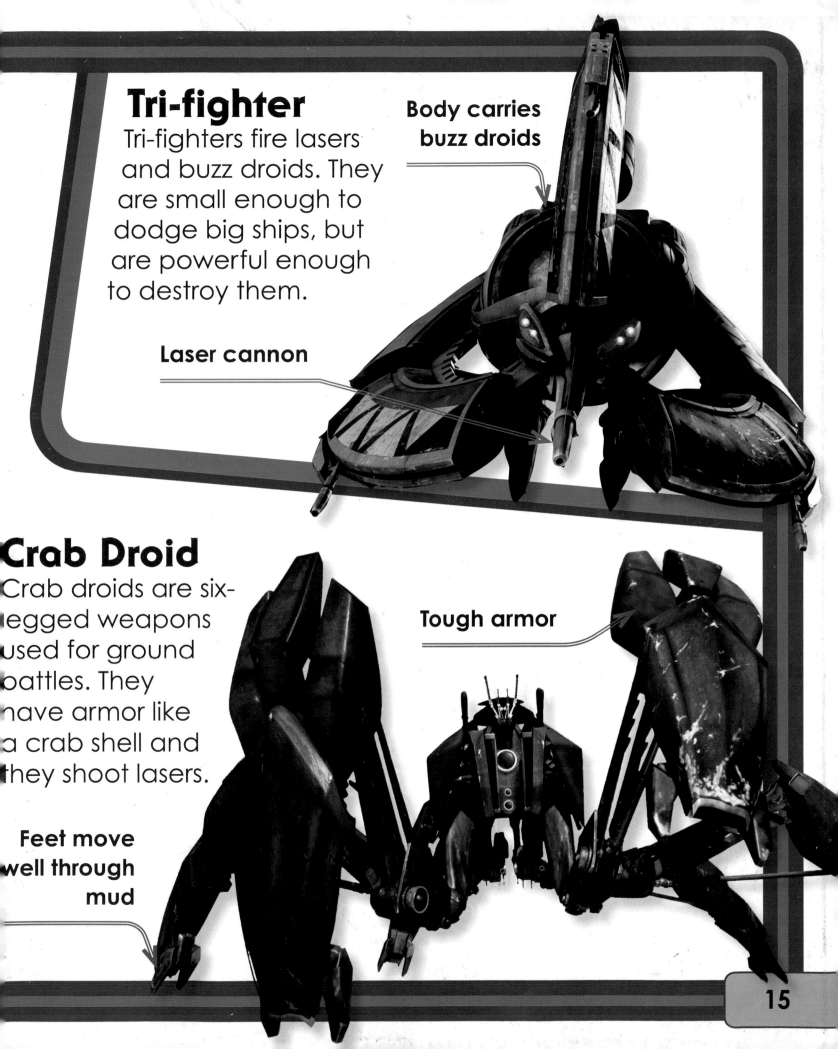

# Tri-fighter

Tri-fighters fire lasers and buzz droids. They are small enough to dodge big ships, but are powerful enough to destroy them.

**Body carries buzz droids**

**Laser cannon**

# Crab Droid

Crab droids are six-legged weapons used for ground battles. They have armor like a crab shell and they shoot lasers.

**Tough armor**

**Feet move well through mud**

15

## Max Reebo

Feel the rhythm with this blue Ortolan. He is Max, the leader of the Max Reebo band, and he loves to play the red ball jet organ.

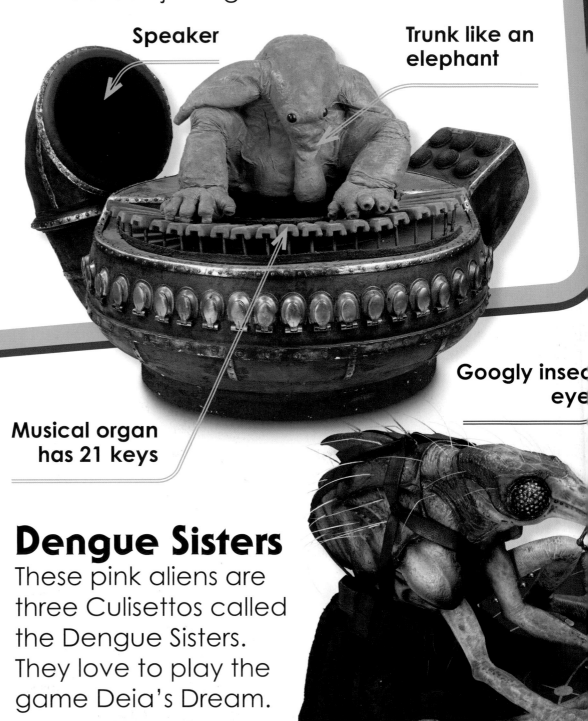

**Speaker**

**Trunk like an elephant**

**Musical organ has 21 keys**

**Googly insect eye**

## Dengue Sisters

These pink aliens are three Culisettos called the Dengue Sisters. They love to play the game Deia's Dream.

Large eyes
have no
eyelashes

Band's
uniform

# Figrin D'an

Figrin D'an plays in a music
band with six other Bith.
Bith are bald, bug-headed
creatures who are intelligent,
peaceful, and musical.

Loose frocks
for traveling

Instrument
is called a
kloo horn

17

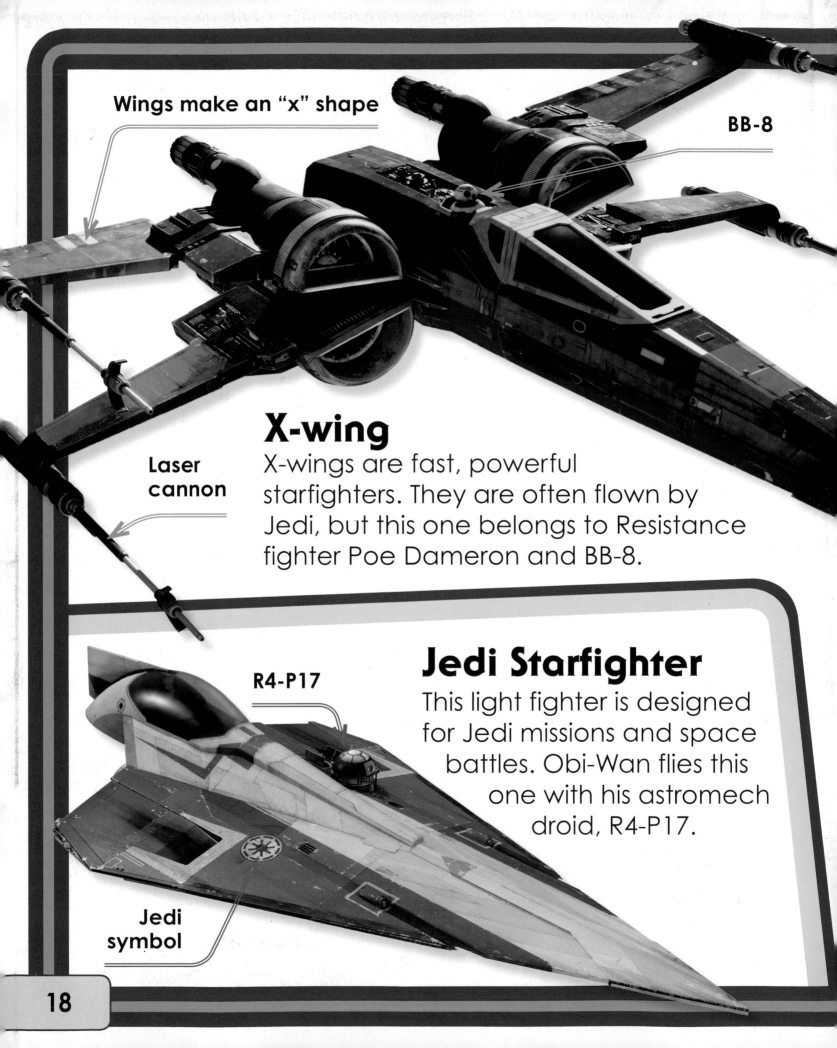

**Wings make an "x" shape**

**BB-8**

**Laser cannon**

# X-wing

X-wings are fast, powerful starfighters. They are often flown by Jedi, but this one belongs to Resistance fighter Poe Dameron and BB-8.

**R4-P17**

# Jedi Starfighter

This light fighter is designed for Jedi missions and space battles. Obi-Wan flies this one with his astromech droid, R4-P17.

**Jedi symbol**

# SPEEDY SHIPS

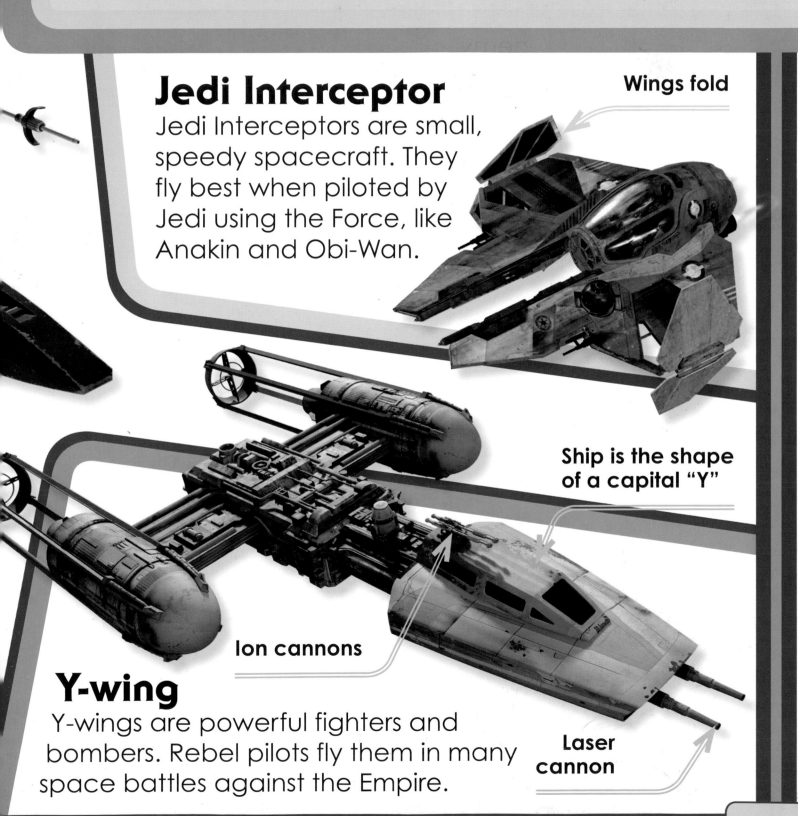

### Jedi Interceptor

Jedi Interceptors are small, speedy spacecraft. They fly best when piloted by Jedi using the Force, like Anakin and Obi-Wan.

**Wings fold**

**Ship is the shape of a capital "Y"**

**Ion cannons**

### Y-wing

Y-wings are powerful fighters and bombers. Rebel pilots fly them in many space battles against the Empire.

**Laser cannon**

# Darth Maul

Darth Maul has been secretly training in the dark arts of the Sith. He is a deadly enemy of the Jedi.

**Chest contains two hearts**

**Double-bladed saberstaff**

**Face
tattoos**

**Zabrak
horn**

**Glowing eyes**

# Gamorrean Gua

These green-skinned bru
make good guards. The
aren't very smart, but th
are loyal and like to figl

**Eyes don't see well**

**Are the Sith real?**

Lift the flap to find out!

**Ion blaster**

# Jawa

Don't leave anything lying
around when jawas are
near! These short, cloaked
creatures will steal it and
sell it to make money.

# FEARSOME FOES

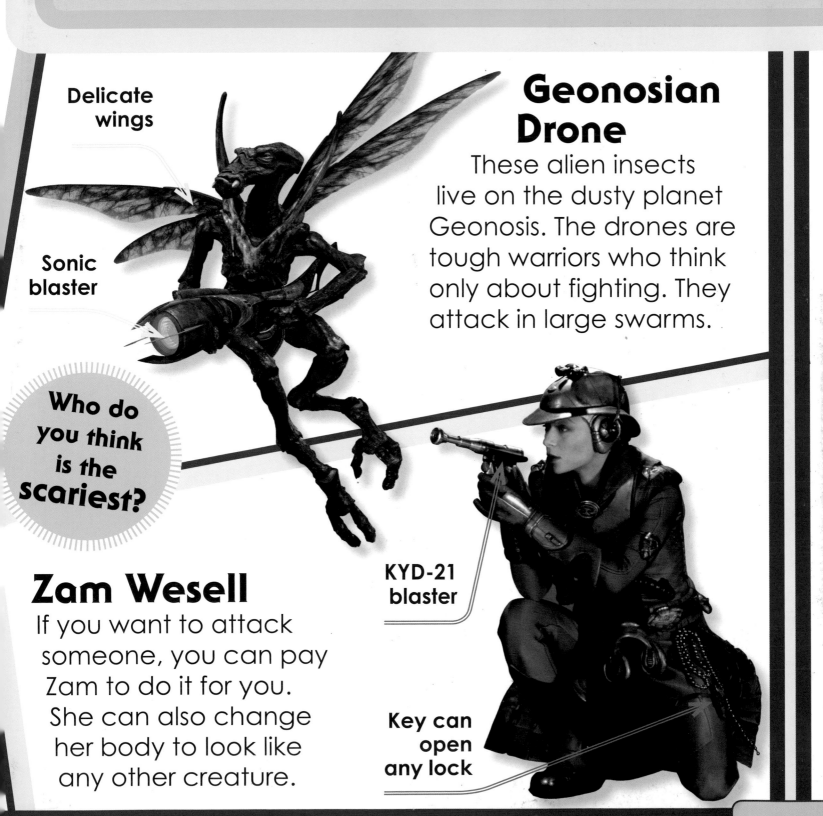

**Delicate wings**

**Sonic blaster**

## Geonosian Drone

These alien insects live on the dusty planet Geonosis. The drones are tough warriors who think only about fighting. They attack in large swarms.

**Who do you think is the scariest?**

## Zam Wesell

If you want to attack someone, you can pay Zam to do it for you. She can also change her body to look like any other creature.

**KYD-21 blaster**

**Key can open any lock**

# Happabore

Happabores look like a cross between a pig and a crocodile. They are very strong and are used for carrying heavy loads.

**Closed eye**

# Varactyl

Lizard-like varactyls can run fast and climb rocky walls. Jedi Master Obi-Wan rides one named Boga to chase General Grievous.

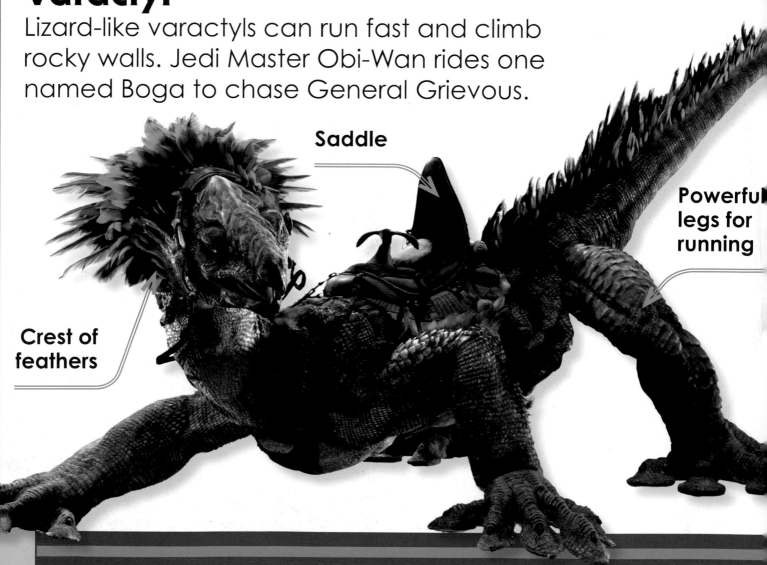

**Saddle**

**Powerful legs for running**

**Crest of feathers**

## Worrt

Squat, spikey Worrts live on desert planets. They hide in the sand waiting for insects to grab with their long tongues.

**Eyelid keeps sand out of eye**

**Spikey body**

**Teeth contain poison**

23

# WORKER DROIDS

**Head contains main computer**

**Long, wide neck**

If you had **a droid**, what would you like **them** to do?

## PZ-4CO

This blue droid shaped like a person is nicknamed Peazy. She provides information for the Resistance on their base on D'Qar.

**Fingers like a human**

## 2-1B Medical Droid

Have you gotten sick or injured in battle? With help from this medical droid, you'll be better in no time.

Syringe

Arm can get longer or shorter

Wide, stable feet

## B-U4D

This loading droid named Buford can carry much heavier weights than a person. He loads and unloads Resistance ships.

# EVIL EMPIRE

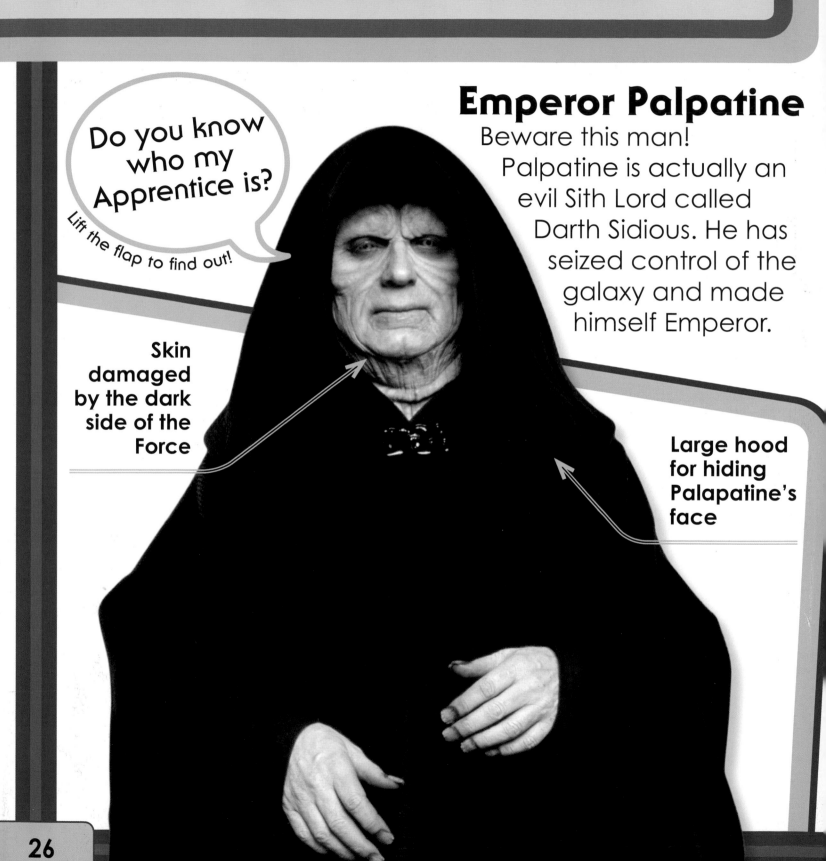

Do you know who my Apprentice is?

Lift the flap to find out!

## Emperor Palpatine

Beware this man! Palpatine is actually an evil Sith Lord called Darth Sidious. He has seized control of the galaxy and made himself Emperor.

Skin damaged by the dark side of the Force

Large hood for hiding Palapatine's face

**Helmet contains breathing equipment**

# Stormtrooper

Millions of stormtroopers serve the Emperor. They are tough soldiers who fight without questioning orders.

**Narrow black visor**

**E-11 blaster**

**Staff for fighting is called a force pike**

# Imperial Royal Guard

The Emperor's best soldiers can become his personal bodyguards. They are also known as the Red Guard because of their long red robes.

Sith lightsaber
glows red

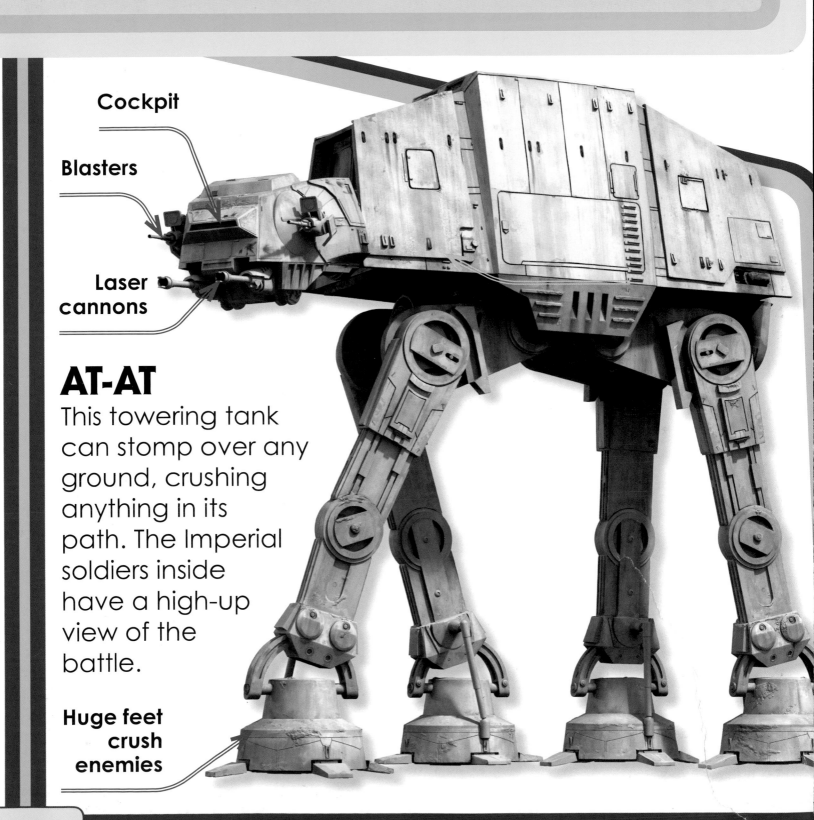

Cockpit

Blasters

Laser
cannons

## AT-AT
This towering tank
can stomp over any
ground, crushing
anything in its
path. The Imperial
soldiers inside
have a high-up
view of the
battle.

**Huge feet
crush
enemies**

# Darth Vader

Darth Vader is powerful in the dark side of the Force. He's Emperor Palpatine's Sith Apprentice, and he's very dangerous.

Would you like to work for Darth Vader?

Mask hides Vader's scarred face

Suit keeps Vader's injured body alive

# Speeder Bike

Speeder bikes zoom easily over uneven ground. They're a fast way for scout troopers to get around muddy planets, but they need to look out for trees!

Scout trooper

Sensor helps bike avoid obstacles

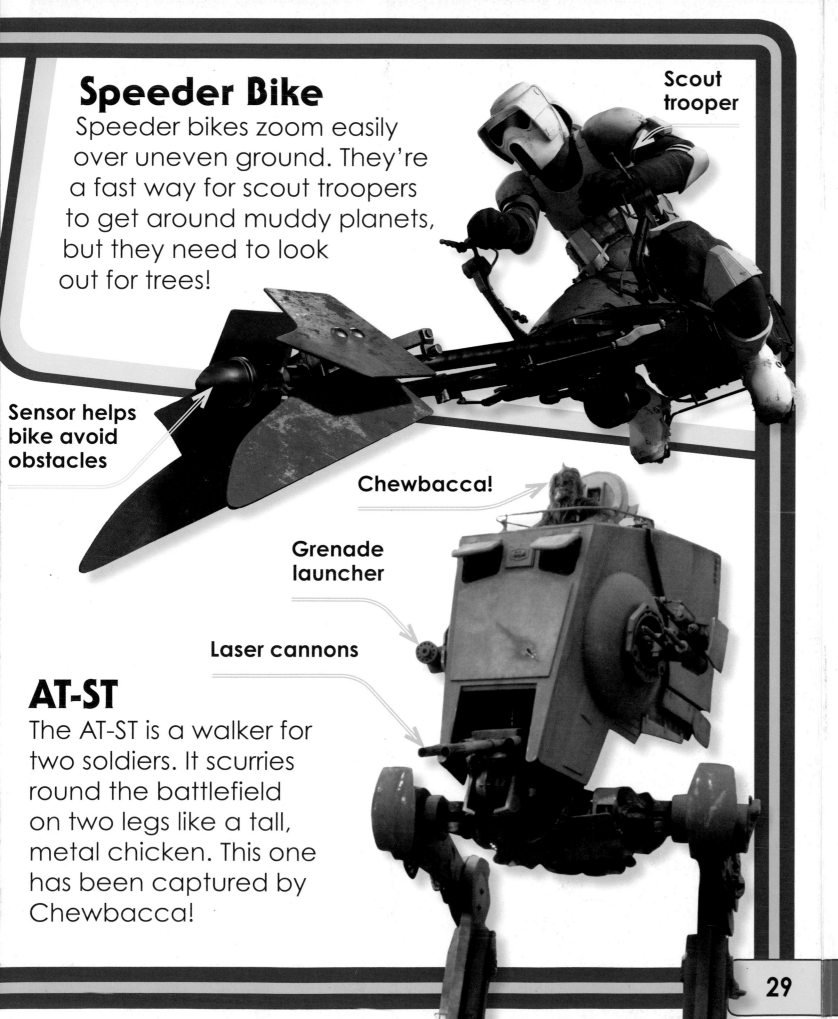

Chewbacca!

Grenade launcher

Laser cannons

# AT-ST

The AT-ST is a walker for two soldiers. It scurries round the battlefield on two legs like a tall, metal chicken. This one has been captured by Chewbacca!

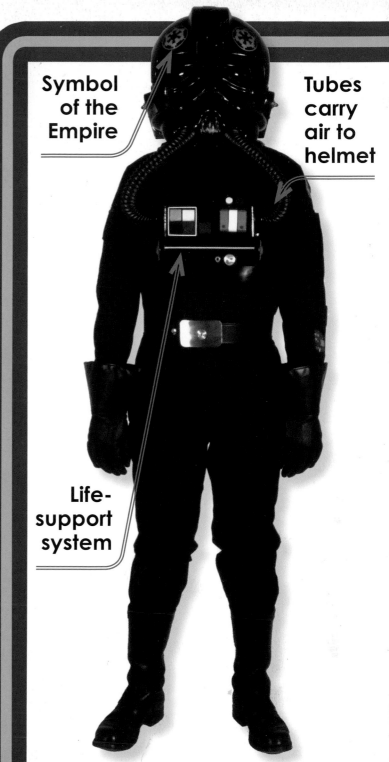

Symbol of the Empire

Tubes carry air to helmet

Life-support system

# TIE Pilot

TIE fighter pilots are specially trained to fly TIE fighters for the Empire. They wear special black flight suits that keep them alive in space.

**Superlaser is a very powerful weapon**

**Building isn't finished yet**

## TIE Fighter

Swarms of TIE fighters fight for Empire. These fast, agile starfighters shoot proton torpedoes and laser fire.

**Panel collects energy from sur**

**Cockpit**

## Death Star

This giant ball is as big as a moon. It's an enormous weapon powerful enough to blow up a whole planet!

**Tractor beam can pull in other ships**

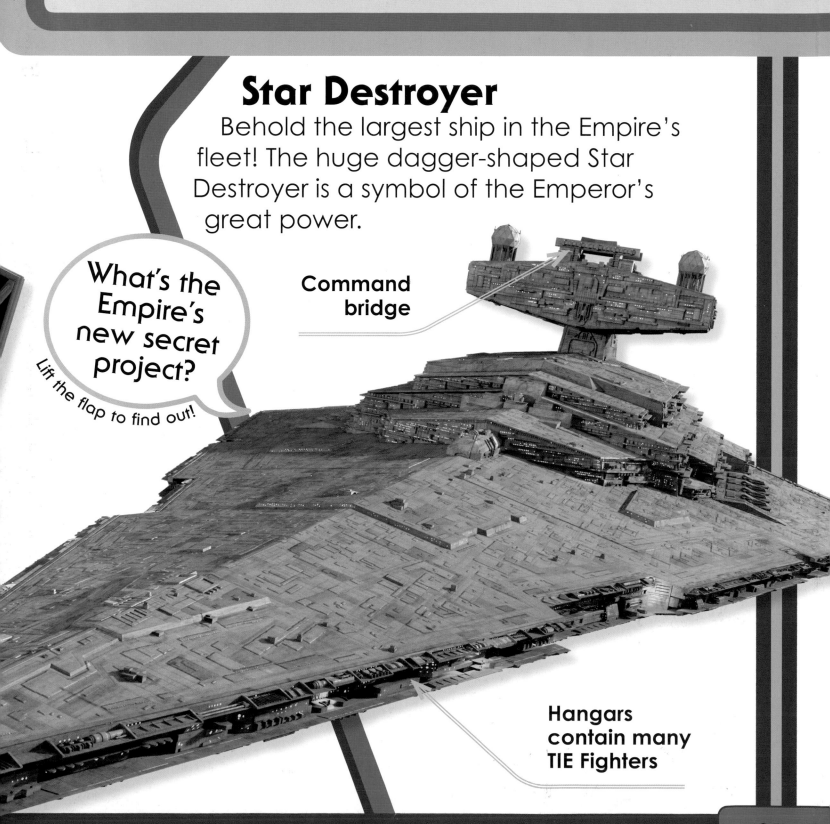

## Star Destroyer

Behold the largest ship in the Empire's fleet! The huge dagger-shaped Star Destroyer is a symbol of the Emperor's great power.

What's the Empire's new secret project?

Lift the flap to find out!

**Command bridge**

**Hangars contain many TIE Fighters**

31

Nose is very sensitive like a dog's nose

# Chewbacca

Hairy Chewbacca is a Wookiee from the planet Kashyyyk. Strong and loyal, he is Han Solo's friend and copilot.

Blaster stolen from the Empire

Bandolier contains ammunition

# Han Solo

Han is always getting into trouble trying to make money. Happily, he's good at getting out of trouble, too, and he helps the rebels.

Gun holster

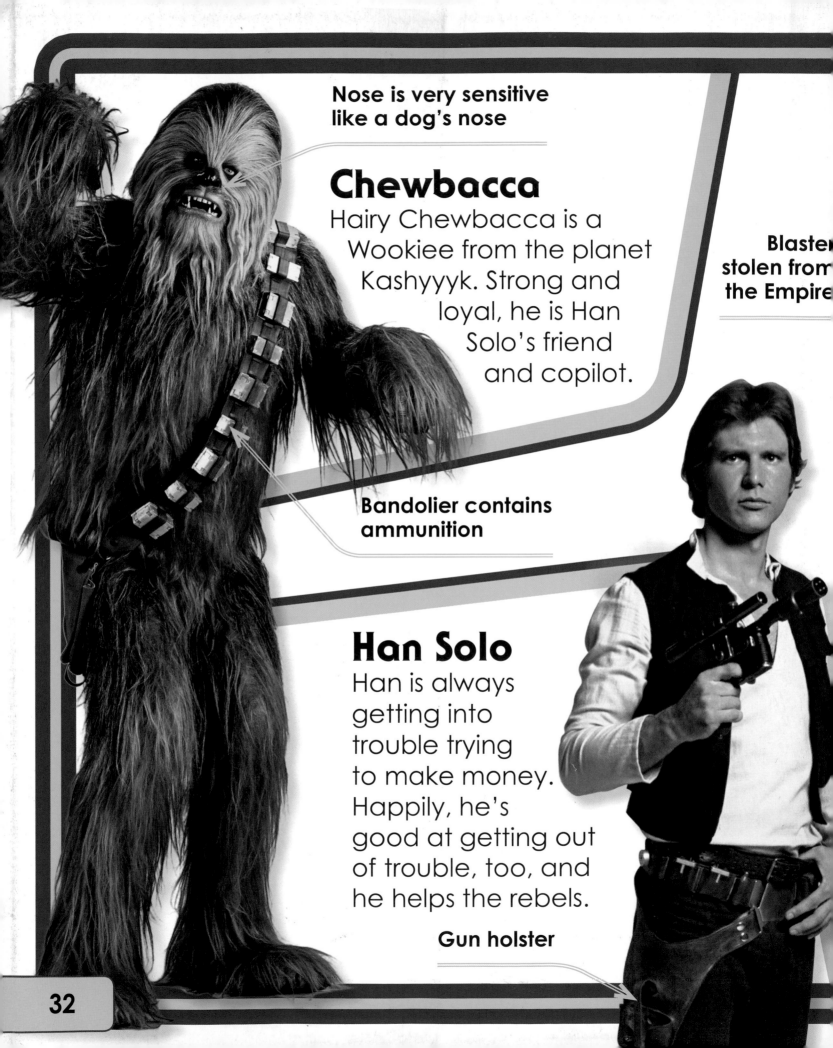

# BRAVE REBELS

## Leia Organa
Princess Leia Organa is brave and smart. She and the other rebels are determined to destroy the Empire.

**Royal belt**

**Lightsaber was Luke's father's**

## Luke Skywalker
Luke is a Jedi Knight who can use the Force. It makes him good at flying starfighters and fighting with his lightsaber.

# AWESOME SHIPS

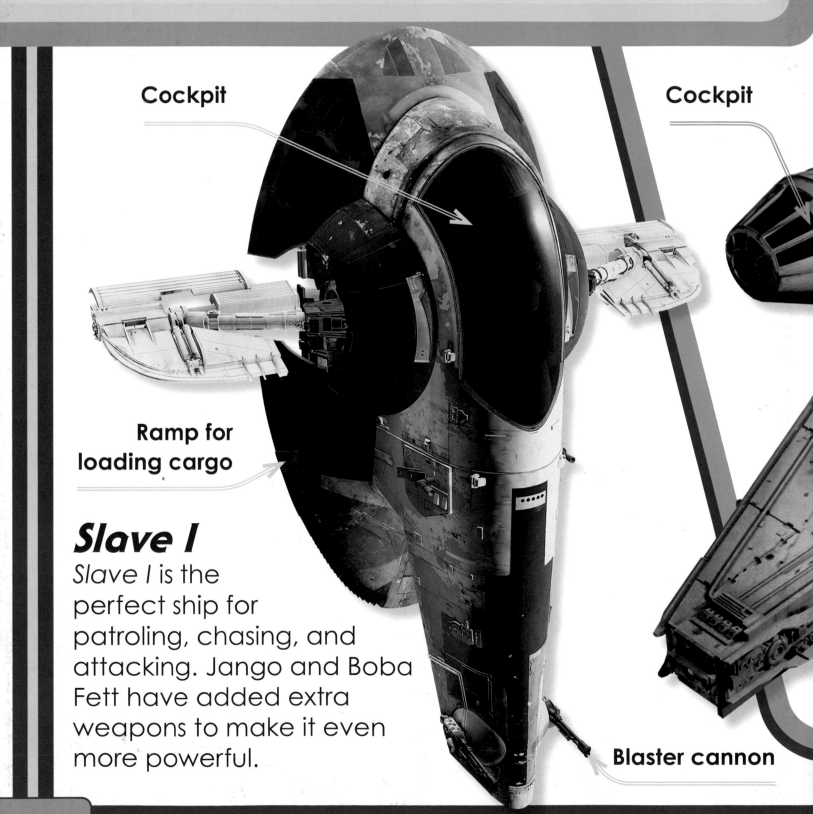

Cockpit

Cockpit

Ramp for
loading cargo

## Slave I

*Slave I* is the
perfect ship for
patroling, chasing, and
attacking. Jango and Boba
Fett have added extra
weapons to make it even
more powerful.

Blaster cannon

# Millennium Falcon

The *Millennium Falcon* looks like a flying heap of junk, but it's the fastest ship in the galaxy. It has helped Han Solo escape trouble many times.

**Which ship would you like to fly?**

Battle damage

# Jango Fett

Jango Fett is one of the most feared bounty hunters in the galaxy. All clone troopers are copies of him.

**WESTAR-34 blaster**

**Sniper rife**

**Gauntlet shoots darts**

**Head contains a computer**

**Short-range pistols**

**Extra-long fingers**

# Aurra Sing

Cruel Aurra Sing is a sniper and can use a lightsaber. She helps train Boba Fett after his dad is killed in battle.

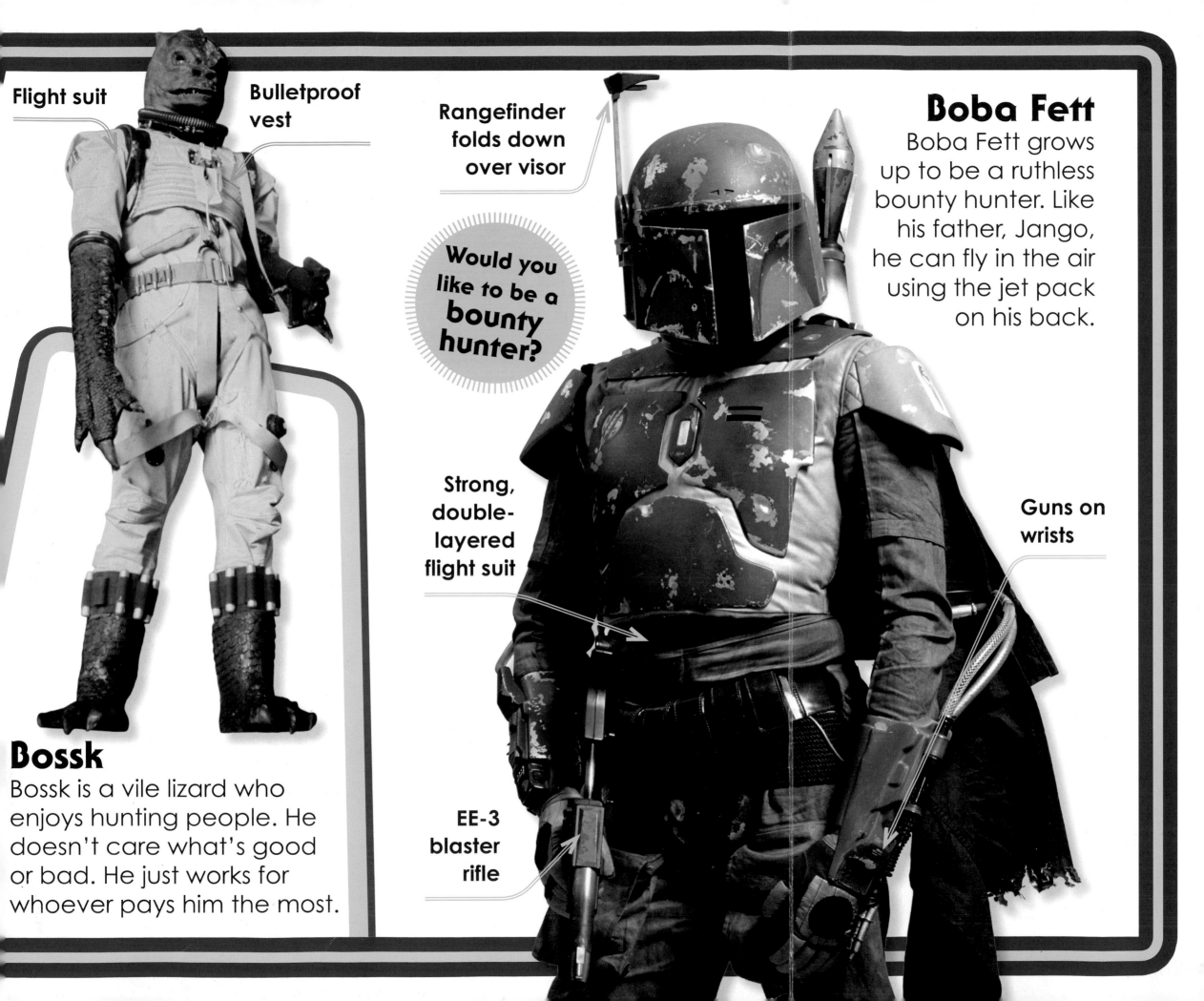

**Flight suit**

**Bulletproof vest**

**Rangefinder folds down over visor**

# Boba Fett

Boba Fett grows up to be a ruthless bounty hunter. Like his father, Jango, he can fly in the air using the jet pack on his back.

Would you like to be a **bounty hunter?**

**Strong, double-layered flight suit**

**Guns on wrists**

# Bossk

Bossk is a vile lizard who enjoys hunting people. He doesn't care what's good or bad. He just works for whoever pays him the most.

**EE-3 blaster rifle**

## Young Boba

Young Boba is learning how to be a bounty hunter from his dad, Jango. His lessons are fighting, using weapons, and tracking enemies.

What will I be when I grow up?

Lift the flap to find out!

**Hands are ready for fighting**

## Watto

Watto buys and sells junk like scrap metal and droid parts. He always cheats people if he can. Watto is Anakin's owner, until Anakin wins his freedom.

**Wings flap very fast**

**Data pad**

**Webbed feet**

## Jabba the Hutt

Jabba is a huge, toad-like Hutt. His favorite things are power and money. Many criminals work for him, and he lives in an enormous palace.

**Body crawls like a snail**

# VILE VILLAINS

## Sebulba

Sebulba loves to podrace, but he cannot be trusted. He does everything he can to hurt Anakin in the podrace, but he still can't beat him!

**Magnifying glass**

**Metal apron**

Would **you trust** any of these characters?

**Coins from winning races**

## Unkar Plutt

Unkar Plutt gives people like Rey food in exchange for scrap metal. He's mean and gives as little food as possible.

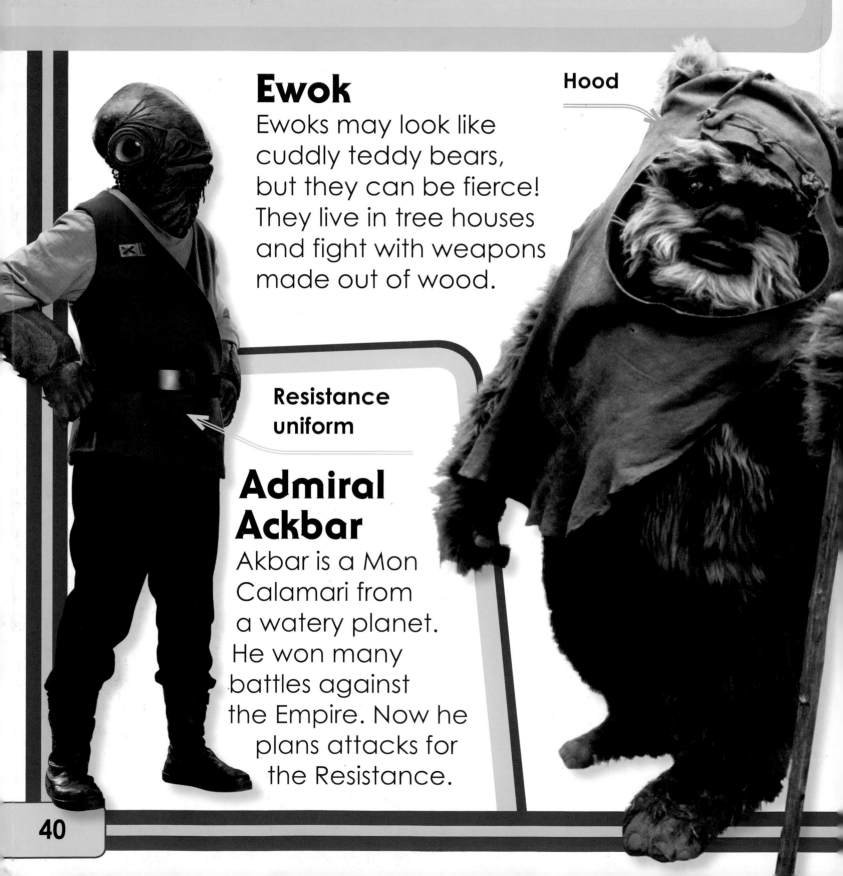

# ALIEN ALLIES

## Ewok

Ewoks may look like cuddly teddy bears, but they can be fierce! They live in tree houses and fight with weapons made out of wood.

Hood

Resistance uniform

## Admiral Ackbar

Akbar is a Mon Calamari from a watery planet. He won many battles against the Empire. Now he plans attacks for the Resistance.

Goggles help
Maz to see

Which
Gungan
helps the
Jedi?

Lift the flap to find out!

pear for
unting

Many jangly
bracelets

## Maz
## Kanata

Maz is a wise, old
pirate chief who
has had a long life
of adventure. She has
a connection with the
orce and is a friend
the Resistance.

Wool
socks
Maz
knitted
herself

Natural
pattern
on skin

# Kylo Ren

Kylo Ren is Leia and Han's son. He was training to be a Jedi, but was tempted by the dark side. Now he works for the scary First Order.

**Rare lightsaber with three blades**

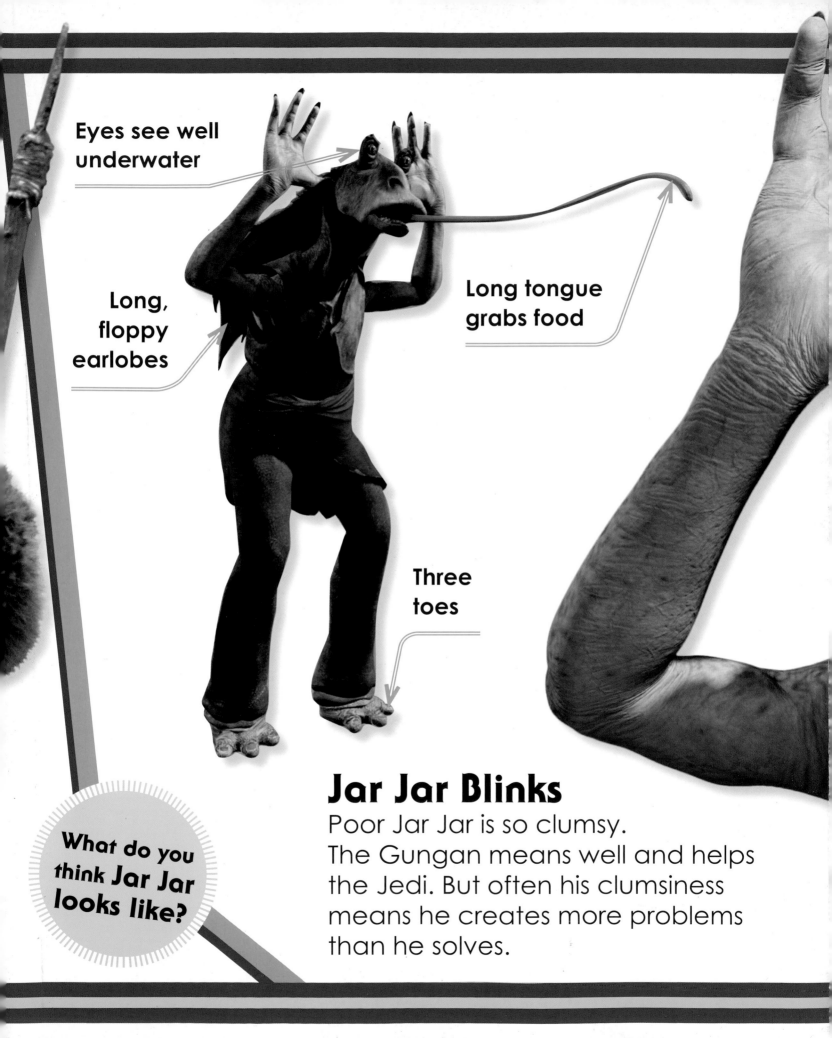

Eyes see well underwater

Long, floppy earlobes

Long tongue grabs food

Three toes

What do you think Jar Jar looks like?

## Jar Jar Blinks

Poor Jar Jar is so clumsy. The Gungan means well and helps the Jedi. But often his clumsiness means he creates more problems than he solves.

# DARK POWERS

## Stormtrooper

These shiny white soldiers fight for the First Order. They have more high-tech armor than the stormtroopers who used to fight for the Empire.

**Weapon is called a megablaster**

**Blaster pistol in leg holster**

**Silver armor is only worn by Phasma**

## Captain Phasma

Captain Phasma leads the First Order's stormtroopers. She wants a strong, ruthless army, so she keeps a close eye on all her soldiers.

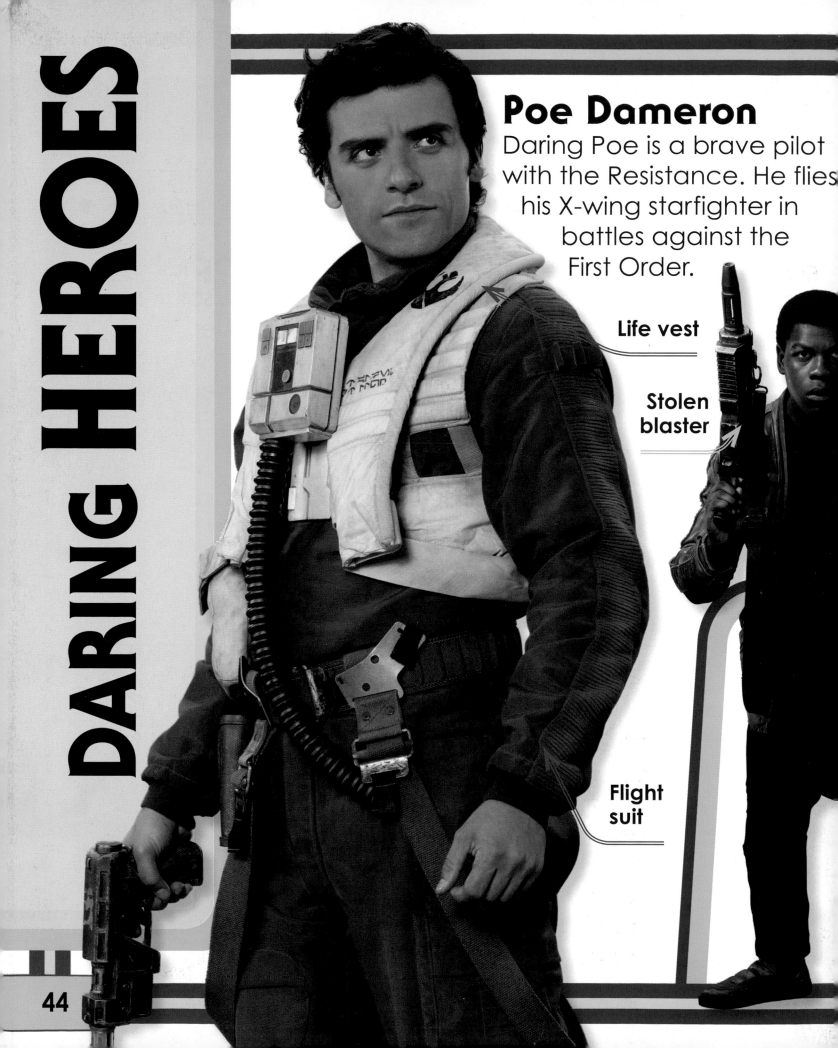

# DARING HEROES

## Poe Dameron

Daring Poe is a brave pilot with the Resistance. He flies his X-wing starfighter in battles against the First Order.

Life vest

Stolen blaster

Flight suit

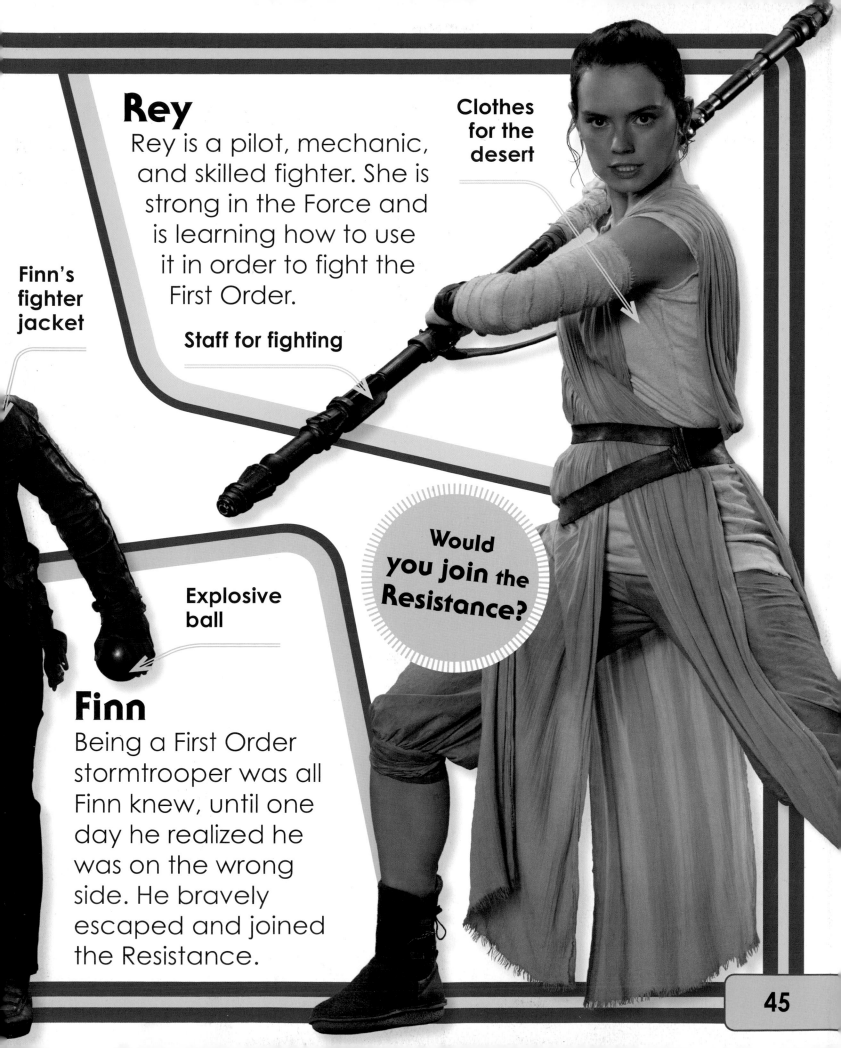

## Rey

Rey is a pilot, mechanic, and skilled fighter. She is strong in the Force and is learning how to use it in order to fight the First Order.

**Clothes for the desert**

**Finn's fighter jacket**

**Staff for fighting**

**Explosive ball**

**Would you join the Resistance?**

## Finn

Being a First Order stormtrooper was all Finn knew, until one day he realized he was on the wrong side. He bravely escaped and joined the Resistance.

**1** Who is the most powerful Jedi?

**2** Who is Anakin's Jedi Master?

**3** What color are the markings on ARC trooper armor?

**4** How many arms does General Grievous have?

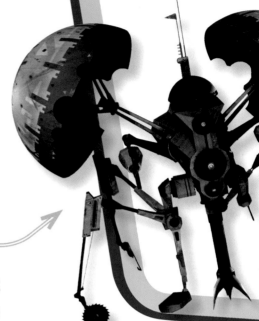

**5** What is this?

**6** What color is Max Reebo?

**7** Which droid flies in Poe's X-wing?

**8** Who has been secretly training in the dark arts of the Sith?

**9** What is the name of the varactyl ridden by Obi-Wan Kenobi?

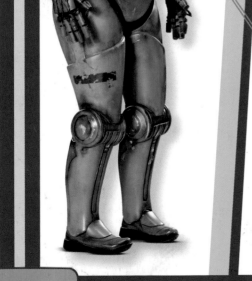

**10** Who is this?

**11** What color robes do the Emperor's bodyguards wear?

**12** What type of bird does an AT-ST look like?

# QUIZ

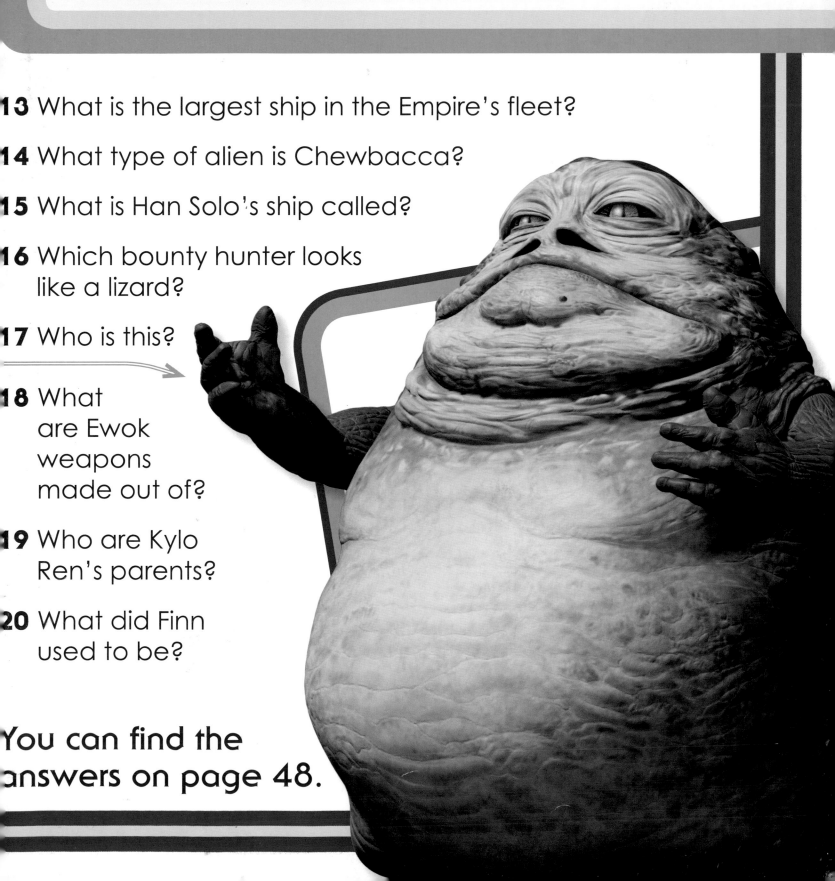

**13** What is the largest ship in the Empire's fleet?

**14** What type of alien is Chewbacca?

**15** What is Han Solo's ship called?

**16** Which bounty hunter looks like a lizard?

**17** Who is this?

**18** What are Ewok weapons made out of?

**19** Who are Kylo Ren's parents?

**20** What did Finn used to be?

You can find the answers on page 48.

## Answers to the quiz on pages 46 and 47

**1** Yoda

**2** Obi-Wan Kenobi

**3** Red

**4** Four

**5** Buzz droid

**6** Blue

**7** BB-8

**8** Darth Maul

**9** Boga

**10** Peazy/PZ-4CO

**11** Red

**12** A chicken

**13** Star Destroyer

**14** A Wookiee

**15** The *Millennium Falcon*

**16** Bossk

**17** Jabba the Hutt

**18** Wood

**19** Leia Organa and Han Solo

**20** A stormtrooper

**Senior Editor** Elizabeth Dowsett
**Senior Art Editors** Mabel Chan, Anna Formanek
**Designer** Anna Pond
**Senior Pre-production Producer** Rebecca Fallowfield
**Senior Producer** Alex Bell
**Managing Editor** Sadie Smith
**Managing Art Editor** Ron Stobbart
**Publisher** Julie Ferris
**Art Director** Lisa Lanzarini
**Publishing Director** Simon Beecroft

**Written by Elizabeth Dowsett**

First American Edition, 2016
Published in the United States by DK Publishing
345 Hudson Street, New York,
New York 10014

Page design copyright © 2016 Dorling Kindersley Limited

© & TM 2016 LUCASFILM LTD.

DK, a Division of Penguin Random House LLC
16 17 18 19   10 9 8 7 6 5 4 3 2 1

001–295424–Oct/16

A catalog record for this book is available from the Library of Congress.

ISBN 978-1-4654-5460-7

DK books are available at special discounts when purchased in bulk for sales promotions, premiums, fund-raising, or educational use. For details, contact: DK Publishing Special Markets, 345 Hudson Street, New York, New York 10014
SpecialSales@dk.com

DK would like to thank Allie Singer for Americanization, Chelsea Alon at Disney, and Frank Parisi at Lucasfilm.

The author would like to thank Emily Dowsett, Reuben Akehurst, Edward Allan, Finn Dowsett, Jake Dowsett, Harry Duggin, Cormac Heinrich, and Audrey Peyton-Nicoll.

Printed and bound in China

A WORLD OF IDEAS:
SEE ALL THERE IS TO KNOW

**www.dk.com**
**www.starwars.com**

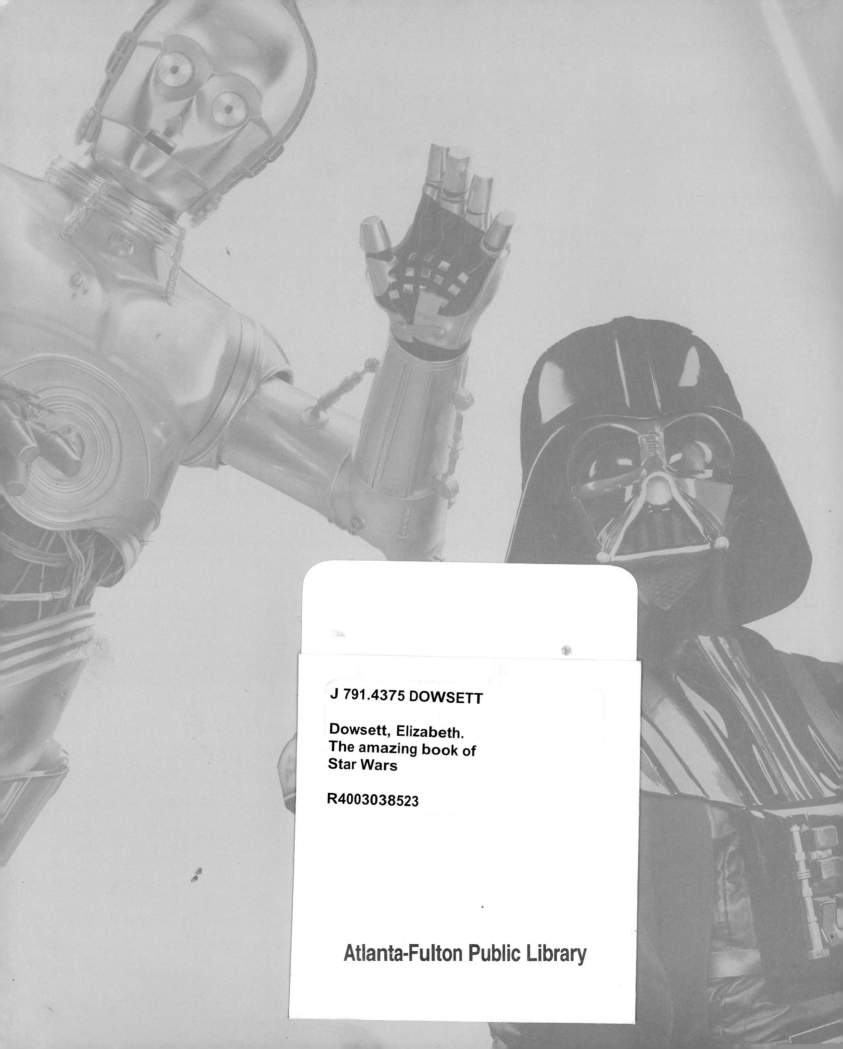